"*The Waves* introduces the reader to a powerful story of the Girl who is consumed by her catastrophic thoughts driven by OCD. As someone who has had OCD in the past, *The Waves* was sensitive, engaging and beautifully illustrated to try and help others understand the Girl's internal world. It captures the feeling of being trapped by OCD so very well, and the way it can distance you socially from those around you. It also helps explain to other children why a child might behave in a certain way. But the story is also one of hope, how to help break the cycle of negative and magical thinking so often associated with OCD. This would be a wonderful book to be used in a range of places, from the home to school to therapy offices. I will start by buying it for myself and my own children."

— **Sarah Johnson**, *Director, Phoenix Education Consultancy*

"I loved this book! It was insightful, well-illustrated and had engaging verses. The subject was handled sensitively, but directly, which is a strength. It is validating to read and the narrative use of waves to illustrate fears and calm was excellent. I liked the co-regulation that occurred between the child and animal-helper, who guided her through her experiences of OCD and intrusive thoughts. The illustrations are beautiful and bring the story together – lovely images to get lost in. I have not read any other books that write about OCD in this way, and it certainly intrigued me. I can imagine this book being used by parents, schools and therapists."

— **Kerry Murphy**, *author and lecturer in early years and SEND, Goldsmiths University*

"*The Waves* reminds us of the importance of warmth, connection and flow when suffering difficulties. Weaving together a sensitive story with beautiful images, *The Waves* shows us how to navigate the big waves of thoughts and feelings."

— **Molly Wolfe**, *Art Psychotherapist, Sandplay Specialist*

"Learning to be calm and 'in the moment' when experiencing difficult feelings such as loneliness, sadness, worry or fear is a really important core life skill that helps us cope with everyday ups and downs as well as with more stressful situations. This set of three therapeutic fairy stories cleverly explains how we can learn to do this through connecting with nature. A truly wonderful set of resources – of value to us all and in particular to those with emotional or mental health difficulties."

— **Sarah Temple**, *GP and author, www.allemotionsareok.co.uk*

T0056266

The Waves

This beautifully illustrated and sensitive fairy tale has been created for children experiencing OCD (obsessive thoughts/compulsive behaviours). With engaging and gentle illustrations to help prompt conversation, it tells the story of a girl helped by an animal-guide to find ways to manage overwhelming feelings and intrusive thoughts. This book is also available to buy as part of the *Therapeutic Fairy Tales, Volume 2* set, which includes *The Sky Fox* and *Into The Forest*.

*Therapeutic Fairy Tales Volume 1 (*2021*)* and *Volume 2* are both a series of short, modern tales dedicated to exploring challenging feelings and life situations that might be faced by young children. Each fairy tale is designed to be used by parents, caregivers and professionals as they use stories therapeutically to support children's mental and emotional health.

Other books in the series include:

- *The Sky Fox: For Children With Feelings Of Loneliness*
- *Into The Forest: For Children With Feelings Of Anxiety*
- *The Night Crossing: A Lullaby For Children On Life's Last Journey*
- *The Storm: For Children Growing Through Parents' Separation*
- *The Island: For Children With A Parent Living With Depression*
- *Storybook Manual: An Introduction To Working With Storybooks Therapeutically And Creatively*

The Waves – part of the *Therapeutic Fairy Tales* series – is born out of a creative collaboration between Pia Jones and Sarah Pimenta.

Pia Jones is an author, workshop facilitator and UKCP integrative arts psychotherapist, who trained at The Institute for Arts in Therapy & Education. Pia has worked with children and adults in a variety of school, health and community settings. Core to her practice is using arts and story as support during times of loss, transition and change, giving a TEDx talk on the subject. She was Story Director on artgym's award-winning film documentary, 'The Moving Theatre,' where puppetry brought to life real stories of people's migrations. Pia also designed the 'Sometimes I Feel' story cards, a Speechmark therapeutic resource to support children with their feelings. www.silverowlartstherapy.com.

Sarah Pimenta is an experienced artist, workshop facilitator and lecturer in creativity. Her specialist art form is print-making, and her creative practice has brought texture, colour and emotion into a variety of environments, both in the UK and abroad. Sarah has over 20 years' experience of designing and delivering creative, high-quality art workshops in over 250 schools, diverse communities and public venues, including the British Library, V&A, NESTA, Oval House and many charities. Her work is often described as art with therapeutic intent, and she is skilled in working with adults and children who have access issues and complex needs. Sarah is known as Social Fabric: www.social-fabric.co.uk.

Both Pia and Sarah hope these *Therapeutic Fairy Tales* open up conversations that enable children and families' own stories and feelings to be seen and heard.

Therapeutic Fairy Tales

Pia Jones and Sarah Pimenta

This unique therapeutic book series includes a range of beautifully illustrated and sensitively written fairy tales to support children experiencing challenging feelings and life situations, as well as a manual designed to support the therapeutic use of story.

Titles in the series include:

Storybook Manual: Working With Storybooks Therapeutically And Creatively
pb: 978-0-367-49117-8 / 2021

The Night Crossing: A Lullaby For Children On Life's Last Journey
pb: 978-0-367-49120-8 / 2021

The Island: For Children With A Parent Living With Depression
pb: 978-0-367-49198-7/ 2021

The Storm: For Children Growing Through Parents' Separation
pb: 978-0-367-49196-3 / 2021

Into the Forest: For Children With Feelings Of Anxiety
pb: 978-1-032-44927-2 / 2023

The Waves: For Children Living With OCD
pb: 978-1-032-44925-8 / 2023

The Sky Fox: For Children With Feelings Of Loneliness
pb: 978-1-032-44922-7 / 2023

These books are also available to purchase in sets:

Therapeutic Fairy Tales
pb: 978-0-367-25108-6 / 2021

Therapeutic Fairy Tales, Volume 2
pb: 978-1-032-11955-7 / 2023

The Waves

For Children Living With OCD

Pia Jones and Sarah Pimenta

Designed cover image: Sarah Pimenta

First published 2023
by Routledge
4 Park Square, Milton Park, Abingdon, Oxon OX14 4RN

and by Routledge
605 Third Avenue, New York, NY 10158

Routledge is an imprint of the Taylor & Francis Group, an informa business

British Library Cataloguing-in-Publication Data
A catalogue record for this book is available from the British Library

Library of Congress Cataloging-in-Publication Data
Names: Jones, Pia, author. | Pimenta, Sarah, illustrator.
Title: The waves : for children living with OCD / Pia Jones and Sarah Pimenta.
Description: First edition. | Abingdon, Oxon ; New York, NY : Routledge, 2023. | Series: Therapeutic fairy tales | Audience: Ages 3-8. | Audience: Grades 2-3. | Summary: Helped by a silver-spotted seal, a young girl finds ways to manage overwhelming feelings and intrusive thoughts.
Identifiers: LCCN 2022053079 (print) | LCCN 2022053080 (ebook) | ISBN 9781032449258 (pbk) | ISBN 9781003374541 (ebk)
Subjects: CYAC: Obsessive-compulsive disorder--Fiction. | Adjustment--Fiction. | Seals--fiction. | LCGFT: Picture books.
Classification: LCC PZ7.1.J726 Wav 2020 (print) | LCC PZ7.1.J726 (ebook) | DDC [E]--dc23
LC record available at https://lccn.loc.gov/2022053079
LC ebook record available at https://lccn.loc.gov/2022053080

ISBN: 978-1-032-44925-8 (pbk)
ISBN: 978-1-003-37454-1 (ebk)

DOI: 10.4324/9781003374541

Typeset in Calibri
by Deanta Global Publishing Services, Chennai, India

Printed in the UK by Severn, Gloucester on responsibly sourced paper

Acknowledgements

A special thank you to Stuart Lynch for all the time and creative support he generously gave to *The Waves*. A huge thanks also to Tamsin Cooke, Katrina Hillkirk, Antonella Mancini, Dr Alastair Bailey and Molly Wolfe for their insights on first readings. Thanks also to our families and friends for putting up with our absences so patiently while we worked on this series of books.

Thanks also to all the children and adults we have worked with across the years who have helped inspire us.

Thanks to the Speechmark team for all their support of our stories and turning them into such beautiful books. A special mention must go to our editor, Clare Ashworth, for her enthusiasm and creative guidance. Her eagle eye came in handy too! And to Molly Kavanagh, Cathy Henderson and Alison Jones for taking our books into production with such care and attention. Our stories always felt in very safe hands.

Hello there,

Thank you for choosing to read our therapeutic fairy tale, *The Waves*. We hope that our story is useful in helping explore some of the difficult feelings, thoughts and behaviours that can be part of OCD, obsessive compulsive disorder. This book might also help you explain some of your experiences to people close to you.

When living with OCD, it can be hard to find healthy ways to support ourselves. Avoiding scary situations and/or using familiar rituals may seem like the only way out. Unfortunately, in the long term, they can also end up making our OCD worse.

Learning to sit with difficult feelings is hard for everyone. If you are suffering from obsessive thinking patterns and behaviours, it can feel impossible. Fears can feel like they will come true, which is why asking for help is so important. If you have OCD, trained therapists can help find healthy ways to deal with difficult feelings, one small and slow step at a time. A plan can be made to support you, with family or other important people by your side.

We hope our characters by the waves can offer their own step of support.

Warmest wishes,

Pia & Sarah

Once upon a time, there was a Girl who lived in a village by the sea. The golden sands and clear waters brought visitors from far and wide. The Girl watched from a distance, as families ran laughing, barefoot to the shore.

"Come and play with us," called the other children, waving buckets and spades.

The Girl smiled politely and shook her head. She preferred to stay by the seagrass, out of the wind.

For what if the waves were to rise? What if they swept away the children and washed through the village and destroyed everything? What if?!

As terrible thoughts flooded her mind, the Girl turned away quickly from the sea.

With a shiver, the Girl grabbed a pebble – smooth and round, with no cracks. She placed it urgently on the sand.

"If I make this, everyone will be all right," she said aloud, laying down one stone after another. "It's up to me to make it all right!"

Concentrating hard, the Girl threw herself into making a stone circle, perfect and whole.

Lost in her creation, she didn't notice the little boy run by with a kite.

"That looks nice," he said, jumping over her circle.

"NO!" cried the Girl as he knocked it out of place.

"Sorry," he called behind him. "Didn't mean to!"

Fighting tears, the Girl scrambled to find her stones. For how could she make sure everyone would stay well and safe? *It was all up to her!*

On her knees, the Girl suddenly became aware of a shape in the seagrass.

"Oh my!" she gasped in shock.

A silver-spotted Seal greeted her, kindly-faced and bright-eyed. With fur that shone like moonlight, it was the most beautiful creature she had ever seen.

"Hello there," chimed the Seal, as if its voice were made from bells and the wind. "Do you need some help?"

The Girl's eyes widened. She tried hard to remember the legends of magic talking seals, and whether they ended well. Yet, if the Seal were magic, perhaps it could help her.

"Well, yes," she said urgently. "My stones... I'm missing a few, and I *must* make a whole circle or else..."

"Or else... what?" asked the Seal softly.

"Nothing," said the Girl, stopping, worried what the Seal might think. "I just need a stone, that's all."

"Well, I do have one." The Seal rolled a stone towards her. "It's rather special."

The stone looked *perfect*. It was only after picking it up, that the Girl spotted the crack shaped like a question mark on its back.

Oh no, it's broken, she thought, about to throw it away. Just then, the crack started to glow a soft blue.

"What is happening?" cried the Girl, as the mark shone brighter and bluer.

The Seal inched closer and spoke gently. "This is the *what-if* stone. It helps show us our worries and fears, so they don't stay stuck inside. That way we can learn how to face them."

"I don't want to face my fears," said the Girl. "Just tell me they won't come true."

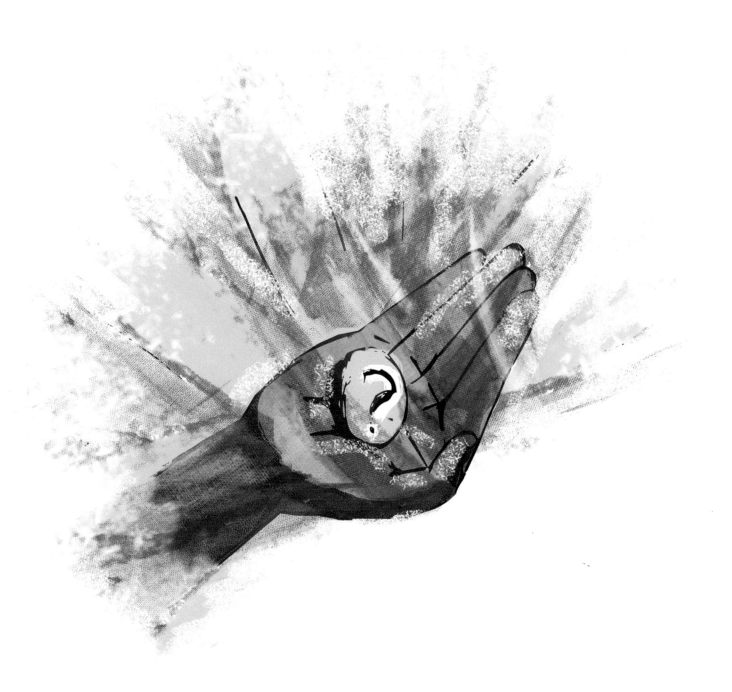

"I'm not sure you would believe me if I did," said the Seal softly and pointed to the sea. "Lean on me and I'll show you a different way."

With the calm, solid presence of the Seal at her side, the Girl looked up and gasped.

Along the shore, waves were lit up with question marks, just like the stone. Before her eyes, letters began to form words, then sentences...

What if the waves rise? What if they sweep away the children? What if they wash away the village? What if?

"Those are all my thoughts and fears." The Girl stared in amazement at the waves, rolling in one after the other. "They are *huge*, and so many."

"Yes, such a lot," agreed the Seal. "So scary. No wonder they knock you off balance. How about we try something different?"

"I don't know another way." The Girl sighed. "That's why I must finish my circle so that everything will be okay. If I don't… terrible things will happen."

"Well… I wonder," said the Seal kindly, "what would happen if you didn't make your stone circle?"

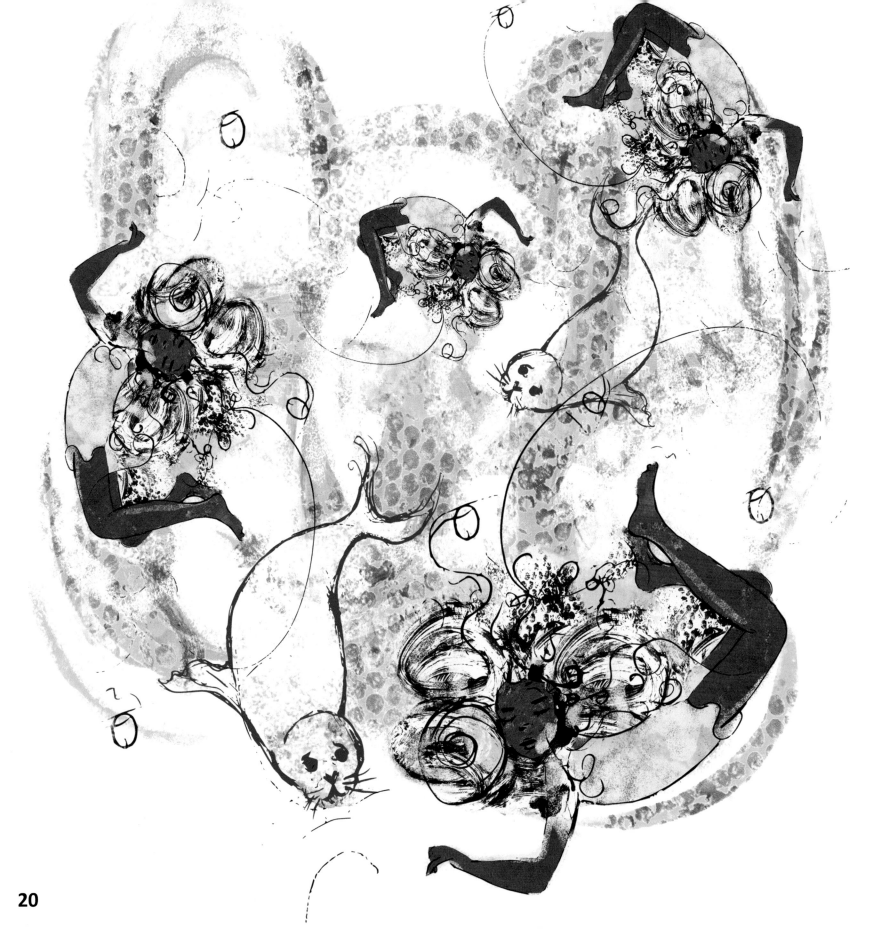

"No, I *must* do it," cried the Girl. "It's the only way to stop all these thoughts and feelings. They are too big!"

"We need to help you feel a bit safer inside," said the Seal. "That takes *being*, not doing."

The Girl gaped. "What do you mean?"

"It's not about fixing anything but allowing our feelings to be." The Seal leant closer. "Let's start by taking a slow breath together."

The Girl struggled to take in any breath. Her chest was far too tight. She clasped her heart.

"Take your time, there's no rush." The Seal pointed. "Can you see the waves... how they rise and fall... can you hear their natural rhythm?"

"I guess so," said the Girl, blinking.

"Great," said the Seal. "Let's see if we can breathe together in tune with the waves."

As the Girl followed their rhythm in and out, she felt her heart slow... just a little bit.

"There you go," said the Seal, smiling. "Can you feel the ground beneath supporting you?"

As the Girl leant back onto the sand, she nodded.

"And wind on your face, can you feel that?" asked the Seal.

"Yes, I can," said the Girl, cool air on her cheek.

"And what else do you notice?" said the Seal.

The Girl looked at the waves. "My fears are all about the future."

"And what about now, what's happening right now?" asked the Seal.

"I'm here sitting with you, looking at the sea, finding my breath," said the Girl slowly. "And even though I didn't finish my stone circle... no-one has been hurt. My fears, they didn't come true."

Slowly, gently, the Seal started to sway, and the Girl did too. Together, they rocked side-by-side to the rhythm of the sea. After a while, the waves began to change.

"Oh," exclaimed the Girl. "Look at that! The words are all still there, but not so big!"

"Yes," said the Seal, eyes shining. "You're learning *to be* with the rise and fall of your thoughts and feelings. They are not sweeping you away."

"And there's something else!" called out the Girl, pointing.

Other letters, faint and new, were foaming on the waves...

Trust. Care. Flow.

Standing up, the Girl raised her arms to the sea and breathed with the wind and the waves.

"It's not all up to me," she shouted, feeling her chest expand.

She turned to hug the Seal. "Thank you for helping me learn to trust myself and life a little bit more."

"Keep the stone," whispered the Seal into her ear. "And remember there are people who can help you. You don't have to do this all alone, or quickly. You can take your time."

After they warmly said their goodbyes, the Girl knelt back down in the sand. She smiled. Stone in hand, imperfect yet whole, she knew now how she wanted to use it… to remind herself she had found new ways to help deal with the uncertainty of life.

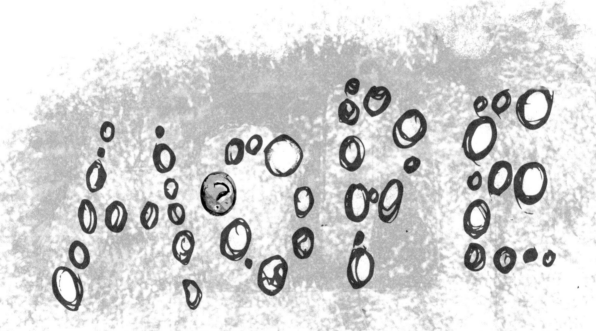

A final word

Did you know that feeling connected to nature can help you feel calmer, more grounded and safer inside yourself? Sometimes finding a special safe place to sit in nature can be useful. This is known as a 'sit-spot' and is somewhere you can return to. The idea is that we feel the earth supporting us underneath, just like the Girl in our story. Sit-spots can be inside too, sitting on a cushion, looking out at a view of nature.

Some people find it relaxing to be by water at a safe distance, be it the sea, a stream, river, lake or pond. The ancient Japanese tradition, *Shinrin-yoku*, Forest Bathing, of being mindful and present amongst trees (with mobile devices or phones switched off, on silent or put away) has now travelled to many countries. Scientists have proven that trees release invisible chemicals, called phytoncides (wood essential oils), that boost our health and immune system, relaxation and well-being. That wonderful smell of pine trees is doing wonders for our body! Equally, evidence shows that chemicals in the earth and soil are also having a calming effect on our body. And it's not just trees or water... it can be hills, heathland, rocks, flowers, cloud-watching, that can make us feel calmer inside ourselves.

As many of us live in towns and cities, finding a little corner of nature can work well. Please make sure that if you do explore spaces outside, you stay safe, that there are trusted people nearby, and/or people know where you have gone. And if you don't have access to nature, looking at pictures can help too!

Your teachers and parents/caregivers can find out more about the idea of nature as a support for well-being in our book *Rewilding Children's Imaginations*, which is packed full of creative ideas of how to connect with nature in fun, safe ways, through art making, storytelling and folktales.

We hope that you can find nature a support and resource in times of difficulty.

Pia & Sarah

Therapeutic Fairy Tales Volume 2:

Therapeutic Fairy Tales Volume 1:

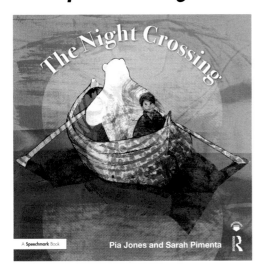

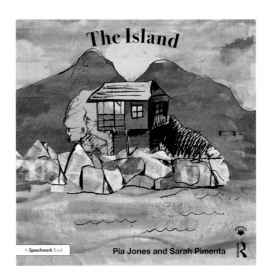